The Deep End of Poetry

Faith Niebaum

The Deep End of Poetry © 2022 Faith Niebaum

Presentation by *BookLeaf Publishing*

Web: www.bookleafpub.com

E-mail: info@bookleafpub.com

ISBN: 9789395950947

First edition 2022

This poetry book is definitely dedicated to my mom, my son Malcolm and his father who is also the love of my life, Joey. They all have a tight hold on my soul.

ACKNOWLEDGEMENT

I think if we all just breathe it'll be okay. But even that seems hard to do some days! Let's take a dive into the deep end of poetry and see how much we relate.

PREFACE

I just want people to read my poetry. The ones who need it the most.

Flowers

Beautiful things grow from inside the earth.
Surrounded and buried beneath a cold dark place
we call, dirt.

Growth comes from days it's been pouring down
rain.
Open the curtain by the windowpane.
We never let any light in, so the darkness
remains.

Inside of our minds is filled with endless doubt.
Gotta water yourself to get out of this drought.
Remember the sun shine is right behind the
clouds.

Rhymes

Inside the light of a wishful thinking mind -
you will find a dim concept of life. Even tho we
strive to feel more alive we still have losses
caught between run, go numb and hide.
Flip the switch- rewrite your life script. Maybe
then you can fit happiness and bliss and feel a
bit more adequate.

I'll help fill your life with colors. Because even
when it all seems grey, I'll be here to take it
away. It's never too late to find the gold- it's
straight up the road leading down the rainbow.

I pray you see life's colors inside your beautiful
mind.
I'd even give you my eyes if you ever went
blind.
Got my heart tied in a bind and now I'm blind to
the darker side of life. Finally feeling more than
alright.

Fuck a wine and dine my soul and mind need to
be 69'd
How come the realest signs always have the
shortest line?

Focus on life's beauty instead of the pain. You'll open yourself up to a whole new lane so you you don't have to keep up, slow down or have a steady pace. Its up to you to be true to the daily dont's and do's.
Only one that can change your life is the mirrors reflection looking back at you.

Voice of a whisper

The air is turning crisper
Time to call and say that
You missed her

Fresh air and a deep breath
Don't hold things in for too long
Might cause your own death

Tragically repeating patterns unconsciously
Lie to yourself and say you'd be proud of me
You wouldn't
Not today nor the one that just passed
Fucking up my life just to feel more like trash

Soak it up now cause todays already late
School of hard knocks I sure did not graduate

Fuck the past , we all say that
But technically speaking we're living our future
selves past.
Are we trapped ?
Yes
Absolutely we are
Will we ever move forward with the end of
despair

Alive today but again here we are drowning and
it's not even that deep
Today will be ending and looked down upon
Then tomorrow you'll blink and now the day
after is gone
Patterns overlapping like a worn out shitty song
You'll repeat it forever till it just seems too long

Broken record of life
Just gotta find where you belong
Nothing that's right will ever feel wrong

Days

The days I once lived in were so dark and
gloomy.
No body cared and no body knew me.
I think in my head- I just wanted to be saved; so
a new road I paved.

Negativity started filling my mind one day.
I dug myself a metaphorical grave.

It was a space I promised I would not stay

the black hole started turning grey
I was slowly breaking away

Freedom began when I created a new pathway,
now negatives that once filled my mind - are at
bay.

Tripping

I know that life won't ever be perfect but at least we're trying to find the purpose. I guess we learned it has to come within. Within yourself; you'll find again. I guess looking up is always better. Whether the weather decides to be Sunny or a cloudy day, it's all beautiful when you say my name. Don't be tripping on the shit that has you daydreaming. I could write 1 million poems and you'll still wont know the meaning. emotions really are so deceiving. You're the drug that has me Pfening. for you I will forever be pleasing. you give me a really good feeling plus you have the light inside of me beaming. when I cry your shoulder I'll be leaning on. We could go on and on about things we've done. Of course the walk of life turns to a run. never knew I was good at saying puns. born on the seventh day so I have some luck. I can Fuck and make love. you're like an angel from above even though you don't believe in that stuff. Youll forever be enough. I think everything will be just fine but we all need change so good thing I'm a dime.

Wings against Horns

All my life it seems to be, there's an Angel and a Devil sitting on each side of me. I've been wondering how much longer it will be till I can see the brighter side of things. I guess I figured out why my ears always ring. I know that it is them, even tho I cannot see, I still hear the whispering always saying something sweet. In the other ear all I hear is all the screams. Maybe thats why I'm always burning up or freezing- Probably from the feeling of hot breath blow my hair while saying that no body cares. And even though that life's not fair, I gotta keep on moving on so I can see what it'll bring. Till then I'll float up in air just like the Angel who found it's wings.

Tide of untitled

Riddled with anxiety
Constantly struggling not to assume that
everybody in the room is speaking foul of me
Or mad at me
It's maddening

Ive tried to turn on the lights in this little life of
mine

Pin me down like a city on a map
Remember saying one day we would do that?
It's just a dream we've always had

Emotions of mine always unraveling

Well my wandering brains the only thing that's
been traveling

Feels like there's no one listening
I'm always blabbering
I snap a lot sometimes
All of the time
I try to rhyme cause it helps pass
The time while alone I sit
I'm alwaus pondering "why"

Why couldn't the Candid happiness be the only
shots that I don't miss-
I love capturing the world with you in it
Abominations my second language
Always knew I was an Angel sent from below
so it just goes to show that the emotional roller
coaster ride will always drown you in the tide.

Pretty unstable

Reminding the souls that got detached a long
time ago to just go with the flow
You know it goes to show no one's really at
home
Go find the key that would open the door to
reality that would finally let us see what's really
meant to be
well that's easy,
it's you and me blasting music of all variety
inhaling our vices exhaling built up tragedies.
Let it paint you a picture in your mind and you'll
see that these pictures aren't really chalked up to
what they're claimed to be
Watch and see
Close your eyes and find a tree
Keeping you alive but we're all gonna die
I just want to go for a drive
Go for a walk one of these nights
Losing my sight, it kinda looks like
Im not lost yet Im looking for you
Have you ever looked beyond the shadows of
the darkness
Past the doubt and self pitty topped off with shit
google says is trauma
Did you get it from your mama?

Empty emotionally unstable sentimental
mentalitys got me going mental
Here I am still unstoppable
Crazy and fucked up in the head ?…
I guess that's probable.

Zippers

11:11 when I ask for the time. Wishes come
from inside wishful wishing minds.
But hey, you and I could really collide
We collide and we fight but our love makes it
alright
Nothings too dark until it's light
Outside reactions to inside emotion
Put the cap back on, guess I'm still
misunderstood
I thought bottling feelings and worries was bad
for your health
Release / wanting inner peace with myself
The Happiest homes have sleeping bags with
busted zippers
Grocery sack used for the trash
Filled up with tear coated tissues
Man we all got some fucking issues
Empty it just to fill it up again
Everyone has a story, here's some papers now go
get a pen.

Untitled rambling

Living life one day at a time always come with a
price
What's left to give when we're owned by a
device
Constantly checking and scrolling along
Can't even listen to words unless it's a song
We don't belong
Here
We belong any where
Somewhere in the midst of sorrow and actions
being humbling
you'll find bliss in the abyss
Now don't go stumbling
Try to be careful, the cookie of life has been
Crumbling.
Im sorry I'm always mumbling
It's hard to decide when to fly but I hope you
come with me this time

Patterns

Hopefully I can relearn some worn out patterns
Life gets dark
don't forget the lantern
Where on earth is Saturn
I guess technically we all matter cause we're
made up of matter
Membranes all twisted with things I call being
gifted
Selfies captioned "it's ok to feel tattered"

I love dressing Up In black
But not when we're all gathered
I warned you about those patterns.

———

Here why

I ask for advice but I don't ever take it. I give it my all and I still have to fake it. My life is okay but it could be better; maybe it has something to do with the weather. My sadness arises when I need happiness the most. Most just think it's fucking hormones, but it's not. I have a hole in my heart that drains my soul dry. 6 years past and some days I still want to get high. Don't want to be alone cause I feel so alone. Even with the ones who matter the most. I try and I try and it doesn't work out. But Ill get back up once I'm out of this drought. Nobody knows what I'm talking about. I sit empty inside while I pour myself out. Some days pass by with nothing to spare but somehow someway my soul is still here.

Untitled again

New day
New light
What was left
Wasn't right
Let it go, say goodbye
Choose to leave the past behind
Soon one day you will find
The war inside your mind will die
Along with the pain right by its side
Tomorrow will come in a days time
No longer more, feeling left behind
Troubles will always come and go
But remember not to open what is already
closed.

Shadow of another untitled poem

Burning inside of me is a soul detached from all reality. Constantly wondering what is so wrong with me. Dropping pieces of myself into the people I care for the most. Bleed my heart dry by watering others so they feel more alive. So far the only one left by my side, is the shadow that's been with me through every dark time. One day I'll wither and sink into the tide, saying thank you to the loneliness that's always been by my side. The key to happiness I failed to find. Another thing added to things I've done wrong in this thing we call life. I wanted love and to see beauty in things but I ended up blind. Some days I wish to find the key used to unlock my mind. Maybe if I burned all my memories and sadness I store, the universe will make sure to take care of the ones I adore. Today will end just like yesterday did. I'll leave earth alone just the way I came in.

Your mother is a poet

An artist too.
Nothing made her feel more alive than when she
had you.
She knew something was missing and didn't
know what.
A lot of things in life has made her more tough.
Seeing your face light up with pure love, made
her see that she's more than enough.
I guess an Angel was sent down from above.
She will be your protector but let you have fun.
The world is cold but her heater is on.
see your mother, she's just like the sun.

Having you, she finally won
You'll forever have love for eternity, because
you're her son.
when life happens and you need your crazy
mom, away from your troubles you feel the need
to run....

Then I pray that into my loving arms you will
come.

Matter

Mind over matter
Fuck it NeverMind
Negative thoughts feeding on the inside
Pack it up and start to drive
Instead of feeling left behind
Let it go and scream goodbye

What are you trying so hard to find?
Yourself that you lost in a past life?
Build a house and fill it with love
It will start to wither soon enough
Once you know where the problems begin
You can build it back up and watch it crumble
again.

Crashing

Why is it always the bliss that's never lasting
Everything around me keeps on clashing
Remind me of the late nights when we were
romancing
Under the moon, we were kind of slow dancing
No fable stories no we weren't just pretending
Back then nothing even needed mending
It's just my memories and my story I kept
defending
you saved me just by being friendly
I wish things could exist with no ending
Life without living is like love without feeling
Back then we weren't even tripping
Just playing we were higher than heavens
almighty ceilings
Everything seemed to just make sense
-back then
You're the truth I'll never bend
All the answers were written I just didn't press
send
my future is you
don't stay stuck in the past
If I owned the last bit of happiness on earth

I could be burning alive and if I died I'd quickly
shock myself back to life just to survive long
enough to give it to you
Fuck no we're not broken go get the glue
Everything I've ever said has been true
Lost the remote to my soul and now it's stuck on
mute
Never know what to say to you
I wish I knew how to tighten loose screws but
I've lost my mind so what's the use
feelings of madness sadness and doubt
 I've felt a few
Won't let you down
Today is brand new
Rather die for real than to be dying inside
Push me while I'm holding a lit match on a
gasoline soaked swing tied to nothing so I could
get high one more time
The path down the road ain't too far behind
Just take my hand it'll all be alright
Alright
it'll be alright
Come on now open your eyes
No way we lost sight
I'll lead you through the darkness
I see better at night
To all the shadows that have never seen light
The sun may explode but at least it'll shine I'll
find a way to find a little more time

Don't tell me you're doing fine
That's a lie but that's alright
as long as the burden you bury gets through
these hard times just in time for you to have
peace at mind
Never lost
We're just too hard to find

12:34 2:22 4:44 11:11 5:55

I dont remember a time when I didn't notice
numbers
I wanna be done feeling flustered.

One day you're gonna wake up feeling so high
Not on drugs but high on life

Between you and I this is another dimension
External entities beginning ascension
Did I mention
You can learn to relieve all of that tension
Crazier than yesterday
No it's not just for attention
If i had a dick it'd be hyper like me
Id call it hyperextension

Racing thoughts running though my head all day
"Yeah whatever you say"
It could all end today and we'd be back by
tomorrow
It is time you cannot borrow
Make the best of life get out of your sorrows

Lightning

Lighting once struck a cold dark place.

I call it today.
Wish you would just call me today.
Hearing voices in your voice saying faith.

Take what is mine, that's what you told me to
do.
Then take this mirror and hold it right in front of
you.

Reflection of yourself you see?
Yeah that's what love means to me.

Don't you see what's supposed to be?
Didn't we have promises we were suppose to
keep?

Late night wondering minds - yeah we think
alike.

No drug has made me ever feel as high
As the days when I'd wake up waiting to see
those bright earth colored eyes.

Yeah and time seems to fly by
and it doesn't seem right.
But Don't worry I'll be fine
Mountains for you, I'd climb.

Stole my heart, call it a crime.
I get you, even the dark spots in your mind
Yourself you're trying to find, it's alright
Just wish you were still mine

You'll always be mine
Any other bitch, they better be kind
Cause I doubt they'll be able to defuse this bomb
in time.

Seemingly

I feel alone and I don't wanna be
Searching for the love you say you give to me
Maybe I would be better off if I set you free

That's probably the way it needs to be
Rhymings easy when you over think like me

I can see myself and the things I want in life.
Because where I am right now, I sure had to
fight.
Learning how to love myself so now I see the
light.
Removed the things that were blocking my
sight.
I'm not always wrong, im not always right.
But I do know I need to better my life.
No more saying maybe, sure or I might.
I'll get back into the word cause the way I've
been acting is kind of absurd. But that's how we
learn, another page we can turn.

Untimely

Its hard laying down when your heart is heavy.
Even if i was rich id still be broken
I try to keep these demons out but the window is
open. I need clarity, I just want someone to
remember me. Emotions are peddling and its
pretty unsettling when you cant make up your
mind and were running out of time so fuck this.
Im sad but could be sadder. Im broke and could
be broker. Im trying but ill try harder. Ill live
until the world gets smaller. Im trapped up in my
mind and I aint got no place to go. The
overwhelming sadness takes over my whole
body mind and soul.

Printed in the USA
CPSIA information can be obtained
at www.ICGtesting.com
LVHW011228270324
775600LV00011B/423